McKenzie River

Goodpasture Bridge.

McKenzie River

Deke Meyer

GOODPASTURE BRIDGE
BUILT BY
LANE CO. 1938
A.E. STRIKER BRIDGE SUPT
NO 16-21 29

ONE
TRUCK AT
A TIME
ON BRIDGE

ONE WAY
TRAFFIC
FOR
TRUCKS
+ BUSES

Frank
Amato
PORTLAND

Photo by Tom Gilg

River Journal

Volume 4, Number 3, 1996

Photo by Barbara Meyer

About the Author

Deke Meyer is a full-time freelancer from Monmouth, Oregon, where he lives with his wife Barbara, who also fly fishes.

His articles have been featured in most of the major fly fishing and outdoor magazines. His previous books include *Float Tube Fly Fishing*, *Advanced Fly Fishing For Steelhead*, *Saltwater Flies: Over 700 of the Best*, *Tying Trout Flies: 12 of the Best*, *Tying Trout Nymphs: 12 of the Best*, and *Tying Bass Flies: 12 of the Best*.

If you have any comments or would like to write to the author, he can be reached through the publisher at the following address:

Deke Meyer c/o Frank Amato Publications, Inc.
PO Box 82112
Portland, OR 97282

◆

Acknowledgments

The author would like to thank the following folks for their help with this book: Chris Daughters, Allan Cline, Rod Johnson, Jeff Ziller, Bob Spencer, Don McNeil, Denise Trowbridge, Cal Hudspeth, Brian O'Keefe, Gene and Virginia Trump and Tom Gilg.

◆

Series Editor: Frank Amato—Kim Koch

Subscriptions:
Softbound: $35.00 for one year (four issues)
$65.00 for two years
Hardbound Limited Editions: $95.00 one year, $170.00 for two years

Design: Alan Reid
Photography: Deke Meyer (unless otherwise noted)
Cover photo: Brian O'Keefe   **Back cover photo:** Deke Meyer
Fly plates by: Jim Schollmeyer
Map: Alan Reid
Printed in Hong Kong
Softbound ISBN:1-57188-053-4, Hardbound ISBN:1-57188-054-2
(Hardbound Edition Limited to 500 Copies)

McKenzie River

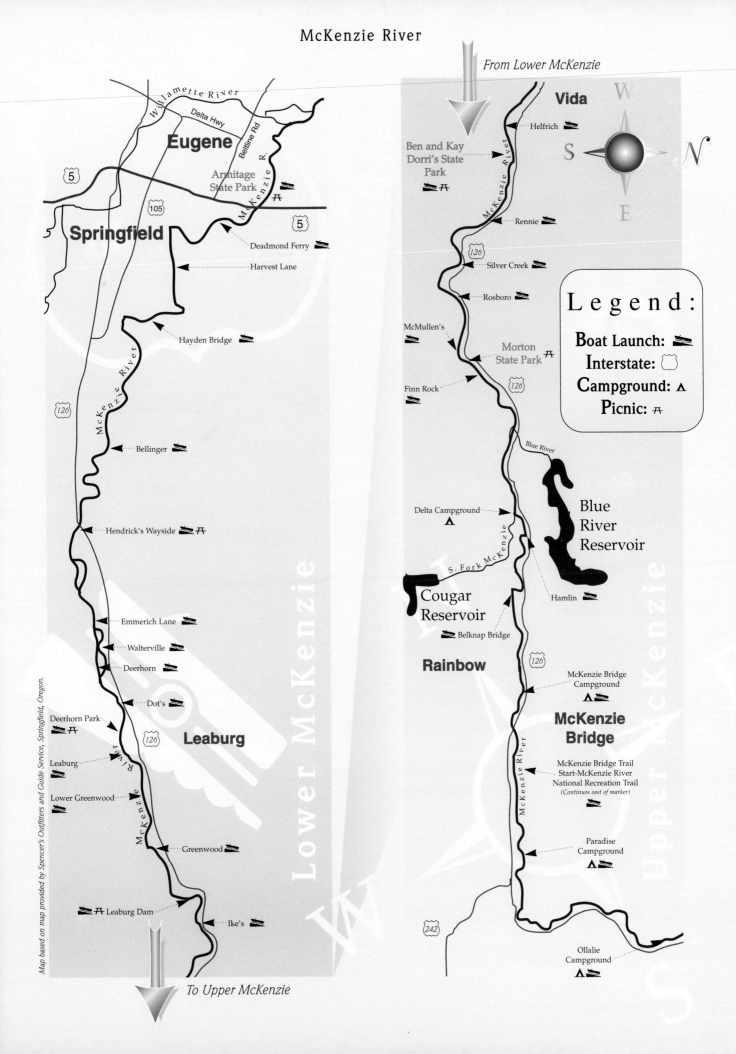

From Lower McKenzie

Vida

Helfrich

Ben and Kay
Dorri's State
Park

Rennie

Silver Creek

Rosboro

McMullen's

Morton
State Park

Finn Rock

Blue River

Legend:

Boat Launch:
Interstate:
Campground: ⅄
Picnic: ⊼

Delta Campground

**Blue
River
Reservoir**

S. Fork McKenzie

Hamlin

**Cougar
Reservoir**

Belknap Bridge

Rainbow

McKenzie Bridge
Campground

**McKenzie
Bridge**

McKenzie Bridge Trail
Start-McKenzie River
National Recreation Trail
(Continues east of marker)

Paradise
Campground

242

Ollalie
Campground

Willamette River

Delta Hwy

Belline Rd

Eugene

McKenzie R.

5

Armitage
State Park

105

Springfield

5

Deadmond Ferry

Harvest Lane

Hayden Bridge

McKenzie River

126

Bellinger

Hendrick's Wayside

Emmerich Lane

Walterville

Deerhorn

Dot's

Deerhorn Park

126

Leaburg

Leaburg

Lower Greenwood

McKenzie River

Greenwood

Leaburg Dam

Ike's

To Upper McKenzie

Lower McKenzie

Upper McKenzie

Map based on map provided by Spencer's Outfitters and Guide Service, Springfield, Oregon.

Then there are those wonderful afternoons when everything seems to be perfect: mayflies hatch, trout rise, and you're on the stream.

McKenzie River

When the Cascade Mountains came to be, by a shrugging of the shoulders of massive tectonic plates beneath Mother Earth, volcanoes erupted, splattering ash, pumice, dust and boulders into the sky, to later fall to the ground. Lava squirted and rolled, undulating as hissing liquid rock snakes that redefined the ground. Much later, rocks and ground cooled and the McKenzie River flowed, flavored forever by microscopic bits of minerals conducive to growing aquatic plants and animals. Of these, the fly fisher finds primary significance in nymphs, sculpins, minnows and our beloved trout.

Cutthroat were native to the river, and probably rainbow, but hatchery plantings have disturbed the tracings of genetic trout heritage, particularly with rainbow. There is a strong population of wild rainbow, with more numbers of wild cutthroat in the lower river. The McKenzie hosts a small but stable population of bull trout. Current regulations require that all wild trout be returned to the McKenzie River unharmed. McKenzie trout average 8-14 inches, with some going 16 inches, and an occasional fish 18 inches or better. Many of the larger rainbow exhibit the same dark coloration and deep red stripe that Deschutes rainbow do, and proudly bear the same moniker, "redside". However, the McKenzie is not a trophy trout river.

Steelhead in any number are not native to the McKenzie, although it's possible these migratory rainbow established remnant colonies because steelhead go upriver to spawn, instituting new runs in an evolutionary fashion. Since biologists estimate that some 400 to 1,000 steelhead now spawn in the wild in the McKenzie system, we can guess that eons ago there may have been some native steelhead in the McKenzie watershed, although whether they could negotiate the Willamette Falls is unknown. From a yearly release of 108,000 smolts, there is now a modest hatchery summer steelhead run of 2,000 to 3,000 adult fish that spend two years in the ocean and run

McKenzie trout average 8-14 inches, with some going 16 inches, and an occasional fish 18 inches or better.
The McKenzie is not a trophy trout river.

The McKenzie is a classic Pacific Northwest semi-rainforest river. It runs blue-green where the river canyon squeezes tumbling runs between boulder-strewn pockets.

from 7 to 9 pounds, with an occasional three-salt fish that weighs 12 or 13 pounds. While some continue upstream and spawn in the McKenzie system, most pause at Leaburg Dam, which is somewhat logical because these fish originate at Leaburg Hatchery.

The McKenzie is a classic Pacific Northwest semi-rainforest river, cloaked in fir and hemlock, swatted with rain much of the fall, winter and spring. It runs blue-green in its upper stretches where the river canyon squeezes tumbling runs between boulder strewn pockets; the lower river below Hayden Bridge is flatter, but can still trick the unwary.

The McKenzie runs close to civilization; the cities of Springfield and Eugene house over 100,000 people; access via I-5 is a quick springboard to her waters. From the March Brown hatch on through the season, the lower river is often excessively loved by its admirers on foot and in floating craft; the water in the upper river is continually churned with oars in the sunshine months. You can still get away from people, but it will take some effort on your part—you may want to avoid peak times and the more popular spots on the river.

In many places the river veers from public access, making extensive stretches of the McKenzie a boater's river. While there are miles of river that are navigable with only moderate boating expertise, many sections are dangerous, even to skilled boaters. Public access offers fishing opportunities at numerous boat launches, parks, Willamette National Forest campgrounds, and along the McKenzie River National Recreation trail.

The portion of the McKenzie below Hayden Bridge is open to year-round fly fishing, barbless hooks; the remaining waters open the fourth Saturday in April and close October 31.

Hatchery catchable rainbow are stocked in the South Fork McKenzie above Cougar Reservoir and in the middle portion of the main McKenzie from Paradise Campground to Hayden Bridge. The river above Paradise Campground is not stocked, barbless fly and lure only. An additional steelhead season extends to December 31, furthering legal fly fishing for steelhead and whitefish up to the deadline just below Leaburg Dam.

I ran across an interesting article in *Forest and Stream* magazine, dated February, 1923, called "The Barbless Hook" by R. Schrenkeisen. He made some interesting comments over 80 years ago that seem to still make a lot of sense, even if he did overlook the fact that women fly fish, too:

"There has been a great deal of talk, pro and con, within the past year regarding the barbless hook. It is safe to say that most of the 'con' part of the talking has been done by those who never had any practical experience with one of these hooks.

"The greatest argument in favor of the barbless hook is, of course, its importance as a conservation measure.... It is by no means an infrequent occurrence when fishing for trout, for more than 75% of a day's catch to be fish under six or seven inches in size. It is also a safe estimate that more than half of this number upon being returned to the water after having a barbed hook removed from their mouths will die.

"Now, the average fisherman who has not had practical experience with the barbless hook, will say, 'That is true and all very nice, but can I hold a fish on a barbless hook?' The answer is that he most certainly can, and hold just as many as on a barbed hook, providing he keeps a taut line. It is true, that to constantly keep a taut line on a fish requires more than a little experience. However, it is only the results born of experience that give any real joy and satisfaction in the honorable and ancient art of angling. The use of barbless hooks furnishes one of the best means to gain this experience, and once it is attained, it will readily be seen that it is possible to catch just as many fish with a barbless hook as it is with a barbed one.

"Another argument that is sometimes offered against the use of barbless hooks is that they tear out of a fish's mouth more easily than the barbed hook. The tearing out of the hook has very little to do with the hook. This depends almost entirely upon what part of the mouth the fish is hooked. If a barbless hook enters a tough portion, it will not tear out one whit easier than a barbed hook.

"Contrary to the opinion of a great many fishermen, a barbless hook has splendid penetration—as good or better than a barbed hook. A barbless hook also hooks more fish. Should a barbless hook get into clothing or through the flesh of an unfortunate angler, it is easily removed.

"When the results that have been obtained by experienced anglers are taken into account, all indications would seem to point to the possibility that the barbless hook will in the near future prove to be one of the greatest boons to fish conservation in angling history, providing it receives the proper support and encouragement from the angling public."

I have often wondered, do trout sleep? Years ago, I clumped down to the edge of the Deschutes River in total darkness, shining my way with a flashlight, bent on filling my water container. The pale yellow beam of the light illuminated a rainbow trout holding just downstream from a patch of aquatic weed, attuned to what I would deem a daytime feeding position. With the heightened water temperature and hopped up trout and insect metabolism of summer, I suspect fish sleep little in that copious outpouring of the energy of life. But what about in the winter?

I can easily picture trout semi-snoozing in resting places in deep pools of the McKenzie, living off body fat or the aquatic insects garnered during limited midday feeding periods when the river allows it.

Of course, one of the limiting factors in trout growth and survival on the McKenzie is the often high, wide and muddy conditions of the winter McKenzie. Trout and insects have a tough time of it when the river "goes out", raising its levels and pushing back into the bushes and trees that line its banks. Trout are visual feeders, seeking prey with keen vision, not easily accomplished in brown water. Insects have a tough time hanging onto river rocks and gravel, let alone feeding on algae and such when the increased force of the swollen river rolls its rocks and silt like dust in a windstorm. If you view the McKenzie in torrent, you may wonder as I do, how do trout and insects survive the maelstrom? But fortunately, they do, and because the fish and the bugs continue on, we may continue fly fishing.

When the river drops and clears, trout ease out of pools and hidey holes, turning to the riffles and flats, searching for insects and slow sculpins. Trout will feed on the available fodder: midge pupae, Blue Wing Olive mayflies, nymphs and duns, Tiny Winter Black stoneflies and the larger Early Black stoneflies. Whitefish spawn in the riffles from late November to early January; trout readily scarf eggs that drift loose in the current.

Many of the larger McKenzie rainbow, such as this one in spawning mode, exhibit the same dark coloration and deep red stripe the Deschutes rainbow do.

January and February on the River

Trout fishing on the McKenzie in these winter months is legally open from Hayden Bridge downstream, but your success is totally dependent on water level and clarity. Typically, the river is up some, with water temperatures in the low 40s. If the river is clear you may encounter Blue Wing Olive hatches in the early afternoon, matched with size 18 and 20 dries and emergers. The winter stoneflies occasionally hatch in February, and trout and whitefish do take them, but it's sporadic.

Some fishermen curse the resident mountain whitefish (*Prosopium williamsoni*) and I've known some anglers who have pitched whitefish up on the bank to rot, much to the olfactory displeasure of anglers who follow in succeeding days. Fossil evidence indicates that whitefish and trout have co-existed in western trout streams for thousands of years—how come we know more than Mother Nature about the proper evolu-

In many places the river veers from public access making extensive stretches of the McKenzie a boater's river. Photo by Gene Trump.

Deke Meyer below Leaburg.

tionary and piscatorial paths a river and its creatures should take? I freely admit that I would rather catch trout than whitefish, but particularly in the winter and spring months I've had many a trip saved by whiteys willing to take my nymphs and dries. Why not just enjoy them?

This probably won't come as a surprise: you'll catch most of your fish this time of year by nymphing the riffles and throats of the runs. One word of caution though: don't charge into the river, wading out and pitching your nymph setup into deep water—you'll wade right through feeding fish.

You have to picture this from a trout's point of view. The fish is hungry, it fights heavy winter currents much of the time, so when the river does drop and clear, the fish naturally ease into the shallower water where it's easier to hunt insects and small fish. And that means that trout will often be only a foot or two from the bank. And even though you may not encounter fish rising to the occasional winter stonefly, the trout are certainly aware of them. These stoneflies are not abundant, but trout do see them often enough to be on the lookout for them, and where the trout most often encounter these insects is in shallow water.

The Tiny Winter Black Stonefly (*Capnia*), size 18, has a black body and dun colored wings, matched with an imitation tied with a dubbed black body, dun colored feather, synthetic substitute or deer hair wing, and sparse black front hackle. A palmered black body hackle makes a workable imitation of the "buzzing" effect of the adult rapidly flapping its wings while on top of the water. The size 10 Early Black Stone (Taeniopterygidae) has a black body and a yellow thorax and underbelly, imitated by dubbing to match, and wings of sooty gray, simulated with a dark gray feather or synthetic substitute wing over dun deer hair, with a black front hackle. This pattern may also include a palmered black body hackle for additional floatation, but this stone doesn't "buzz" on the surface like its smaller cousin.

I've had little luck with specific stonefly nymph imitations for these insects. More generalistic nymphs work better for me, which doesn't preclude the possibility that trout may be taking

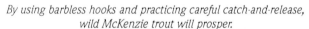

By using barbless hooks and practicing careful catch-and-release, wild McKenzie trout will prosper.

This wild female steelhead was returning to the sea after spawning when her journey was interrupted.

them for stonefly nymphs. Successful nymphs include the Hare's Ear in natural tan, a darker brown version, or olive, the Red Fox Squirrel Nymph, Soft Hackle, and Pheasant Tail in sizes 10 to 14. Some nymph fishers prefer to watch the end of their brightly colored floating fly line to detect the strike, but some type of fluorescent strike indicator greatly aids most of us.

I often use a two nymph rig, varying the size and shape of the flies to better appeal to opportunistic feeding by trout. I add micro-shot to fine tune the nymphs' drift. Tangling of the nymphs is a problem, even if you open your casting loop and slow down your casting stroke. If I find I'm not getting strikes, it usually means my nymphs are not on the bottom. In the colder water of winter, trout just won't move very far to take a nymph, and seem to be tuned in to taking their prey close to the bottom.

Of course, then there are those wonderful afternoons when everything seems to be to the liking of insects and trout, Blue Wing Olive (*Baetis*) mayflies hatch, trout rise, and you're on the stream. Tactics are the usual for dry fly: a nine- or ten-foot leader tapered down to two or three pound test (with a nice long springy tippet of two to three feet long); a size 18 or 20 Adams, Adams Parachute, or Blue Wing Olive Comparadun, dead-drifted over the trout's feeding station.

I enjoy catching fish on nymphs and I know of some excellent nymph fishers who would rather fish the sunken fly, but I have to admit that I absolutely love to catch trout on dries. It's particularly pleasurable in the doldrums of winter, when it seems that successful dry fly fishing is a precious gift, a bonus for still being alive.

*Trout fishing on the McKenzie in winter months is legally open
from Hayden Bridge downstream, but success is dependent on water level and clarity.*

Spring on the McKenzie

Spring announces herself with swallows sifting the air for insects; the swallows migrate from warm southern climates, the insects migrate from their aquatic homes to emerge as creatures of land and air. When swallows arrive mid-March they may find a hatch of Blue Wing Olive mayflies, size 18 or 20, or they may dine on hatching Western March Brown mayflies.

The Western March Brown (*Rhithrogena morrisoni*) is a sizable mayfly, with the earlier duns clocking in at size 12 and 14. Later on, the duns emerge as size 14 and 16. Interestingly enough, that same trend holds true for the Speckled Dun (*Callibaetis*) mayflies that hatch in the high country lakes that help form the McKenzie. The first broods will be size 12, then 14, then size 16s.

March Browns will hatch on sunny days, but they prefer overcast, misty or light rain days, which seems to make sense because the McKenzie has many of those days, particularly in the spring. In fact, the hatches are sparse on bright spring days, but can be glorious on soggy wet river rat days when only the devoted are on the river. River height and clarity only seems to affect dry fly fishing and the predilection for trout to take the duns, and dry flies. Some of the most intense hatches occur when the river is high and off color, too brown to fish but not too chocolate for March Browns.

The Western March Brown nymph is a clinger-type, clamping onto understream rocks by puckering its abdominal segments and protruding gills, allowing it to prosper in heavy current, a common occurrence in the late winter and early spring when the March Brown nears maturity.

It's easy to visualize March Brown nymphs grazing on the algae covered rocks in the fastest currents of the river. These clinger-type mayflies are like minuscule bovines, munching on the pastoral greenery on the sunken river rocks.

Because of their sucker-like adhesion, these nymphs are seldom available to trout in the general drift menu. As a crawling insect, a dislodged *Rhithrogena* is a poor swimmer, tucking in its legs and gills, drifting until it regains the bottom or is eaten by a trout.

You can imitate the nymph with a dark brown size 10 Hare's Ear or Soft Hackle worked along the bottom, with enough micro-shot and a long enough leader to keep the fly ticking along the bottom, where trout expect the soon-to-hatch nymphs to be.

When March Browns are emerging, Soft Hackles are also effective, fished both subsurface and in the film. You'll delight in catching exuberant but not large cutthroat in the flats below riffles, swinging your sunken Soft Hackle cross-current, in the classic wet fly swing. You can use a light rod, a relaxing style of fishing, and just enjoy yourself.

To fish the surface film, grease the Soft Hackle body with silicone floatant but don't grease the soft hackle fibers; let them undulate both above and below the surface, much like the legs and antennae of the natural insect. My favorite in-the-film

This probably won't come as a surprise: you'll catch most of your fish at the first of the year by nymphing the riffles and throats of the runs.

Photo by Brian O'Keefe

◆

March Brown Soft Hackle has a few tannish-brown grouse fibers for the tail, a tannish-brown body (sometimes ribbed with fine gold wire) and natural duck flank feather fibers for the front hackle. I use grayish, brownish toned duck feathers that are "raw" (undyed), so that they retain their natural oils, which allows the fly to float awash in the surface film.

I wanted to design a March Brown emerger that uses the floating qualities of Cul-de-canard feathers, keeps the rear of the fly floating in the film in spite of the weight of a size 12 hook, and one that floats well even after a fish or two had soaked the fly. The Deke's March Brown Emerger (size 12, chemically sharpened dry fly hook) is tied with gray 6/0 thread, six gray elk hair fibers for the tail, a dubbed tannish brown body with the gray elk fibers as an overbody like a Humpy, and with two folded gray C-D-C feathers forming the expanding wings of the hatching dun. Escaping wisps of the C-D-C feathers simulate legs and antennae, as well as capturing air bubbles, mimicking the gas bubbles that help the natural insect escape the river bottom. (When fishing C-D-C patterns, never use any kind of floatant—it clogs the C-D-C fibers and makes the fly a sinker instead of a floater.)

This emerger works on hard-pounded fish, but can be a challenge to fish because it floats low in the water and is difficult to see. To compensate, I often tie a March Brown Comparadun on the end of the tippet, then add the Emerger on an 18-inch dropper from the hook bend of the Comparadun. In

the really hard-to-see-the-fly conditions often encountered astream in the spring, when the sky and the river appear slate gray, even the Comparadun disappears after being cast. I'll then substitute a March Brown Parachute with a white poly yarn wing that I can spot against the gray background. I watch for the quick splashy rise that may be the take to the Parachute, or if the rise is next to it, the trout has probably nailed the Emerger. You'll miss fish, but you'll catch fish that won't take anything but an Emerger pattern.

The Western March Brown dun is a particular favorite of dry fly fishermen, matched with size 12 and 14 light brown Comparaduns, Parachutes or traditionals such as the Dark Hendrickson or Dark Cahill. Once hatched, it often takes several moments for the dun's wings to stabilize for flight, especially on cool, overcast days. The mayfly pumps fluid into the veins in its wings, expanding them much like puffing up an accordion. The dun will often float for quite a ways before its wings have unfurled and tightened enough to gain the sky.

At this crucial stage of the hatch, the mayfly will often make several hopping starts before becoming airborne. Trout rise avidly, slashing the surface.

The body of the fly in the Comparadun and the Parachute styles of dry flies float "on" the water; they are effective because trout can clearly see the fly body in the surface film. With its springy hackle, a traditional pattern keeps the fly body "above" the water. Traditionals do catch fish, and just for fun you may want to use one to dust yourself with a little fly fishing history. However, the traditional style of dry can play an important role in dry fly tactics on windy days. Trout, and particularly cutthroat, cruise the flats on windy days, picking off

◆

In winter trout will often be only a foot or two from the bank, where it's easier to hunt insects and small fish.

mayflies that are wind-skipping on the surface. You can't mimic that action with the low riding Comparadun or Parachute, but you can make the traditional fly scoot or hop a bit, teasing the trout to take it. I've had some great windy days on the spring McKenzie when the trout were in a playful mood, ignoring flush-floating duns and my mimicking patterns, but blasted skittering natural duns and my traditionals that did the same. I tie a traditional March Brown with dun tail hackle fibers, dubbed grayish tan body, dark dun hackle and dark duck flank feather fibers for a wing.

I've only encountered fishable March Brown spinner falls a couple of times, matched with a size 12 dry fly hook dressed with long gray micro fibbet tails, a dubbed rusty body and clear spinner wings, in a flat figure eight style. Other spinner wing simulations include a sparse gray front hackle, with the bottom of the hackle or both the top and bottom clipped. Leaving the top of the hackle simulates the spinners with their wings upright; with both top and bottom clipped, it imitates a spinner wing flush-in-the-film. I always carry a few spinner patterns because on the rare occasions I've found trout rising to March Brown spinners, these imitations were invaluable.

I remember one calm April morning in the flats below the riffle at Armitage Park when the trout ignored the few duns on the water, instead feeding on the numerous spinners. At first I couldn't determine what the trout were taking, because it seemed they were splashing for invisible insects. Then I recalled that while I strung up my rod on shore, I had noticed hundreds of spinners dancing in the air. So when I found myself out in the river, watching these puzzling rises, I bent close to the water, and then saw the rusty body March Brown spinner with clear wings. I ended up catching some nice trout, but finding fish rising to March Brown spinners in not all that common. The trout usually prefer the duns, which offer a more substantial meal.

The second important hatch is also a toothsome insect for trout, the McKenzie Caddis, size 10, with gray wings and an iridescent blue-green body. The *Arctopsyche grandis* is a mem-

*The Western March Brown (*Rhithrogena morrisoni*) is a sizable mayfly, with the earlier duns clocking in at size 12 and 14. Later on, the duns emerge as size 14 and 16.*

ber of the net spinning family, building its lair amid the rubble on the stream bottom, catching and feeding on other insects that drift into its net. After two years it will pupate, then emerge anywhere from midstream to near the shore. After mating, the female dives underwater, depositing some of her eggs on the bottom. While underwater, she breathes via a plastron, an envelope of air around her body. When she regains the surface she will swim or fly ashore, rest awhile in the shoreline brush, then deposit more eggs.

This robust caddis begins hatching in late April, tapering off in June. Trout love this critter, because of its size and because it's so active. Once the insect hatches on the surface, it scampers to the shore, causing trout to intercept it in a tremendous splash. Trout will seize the swimming adult when she's headed to the bottom to lay eggs or on her return to the surface. Because the hatch stretches out several weeks, trout key in on this caddis, eagerly pouncing on the naturals.

To get a trout to pounce on your fly, you can mimic an exhausted adult caddis by dead-drifting the dry, but you can also try dancing your fly on the surface like a skating emerger. The traditional size 10 adult McKenzie Caddis pattern is not complicated: optional short deer hair tail, blue-green dubbed body, palmered grizzly hackle, deer hair wing, grizzly front hackle.

There are other smaller caddis that start hatching in the spring, particularly when the water warms in May. But more noticeable are the first of the cream mayflies, which hatch midday or in the evening when it's warm, starting in late May. When the weather has been mild and the river in shape, you might enjoy mixed hatches of March Browns and cream mayflies. It won't happen very often, but if it does, it will probably be an excellent day on the river. (I cover the cream mayflies in the Summer chapter.)

A popular method for fishing the McKenzie, particularly from a boat, is the two fly method, where you fish a nymph such as a Hare's Ear or a Soft Hackle on the bottom, and a skater

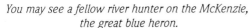

You may see a fellow river hunter on the McKenzie, the great blue heron.

The Western March Brown nymph is a clinger-type, clamping onto understream rocks, a common occurrence in late winter and early spring when the March Brown nears maturity.

◆

dry fly such as the McKenzie Caddis on a dropper. If the trout won't move to the dry, you can fish a Soft Hackle on top and a Hare's Ear on the bottom. The two fly setup can be dead-drifted, but is most often an active presentation where you animate the flies, coaxing the fish to take.

The spring fisherman on the McKenzie will spy osprey gazing intently into the river's depths; the osprey will dive from as much as 100 feet above the river, taking its fish in a tremendous explosion of bird colliding with water. You may feel a pang for the fish, but this magnificent fish hawk belongs to the river and its environs, perhaps more than we do.

The closest I've come to an osprey was a fluke. Barbara and I were fishing the March Brown hatch one spring day when it started raining in torrential bucket-loads. She forgot her raincoat so we hunkered in the streamside brush sharing my raincoat—not too bad if you're good friends with the one you share your coat with. That way we both got wet, but I didn't feel guilty. The osprey was oblivious to the rain, hovering over the river, equipped with incredibly efficient laser-eyes peering raptly into the clear water, searching for fish.

Two huddled fishermen under a drab green raincoat amidst streamside green bushes went unnoticed; the fish hawk hung not 50 feet from us, at a flight altitude of 80 feet. Abruptly the osprey folded its wings and dove into the water with a resounding splash, then flapped its wings while still under water, slinging water in wild spray as it erupted from the river

to fly away with a six inch fish clutched in its talons.

On a quieter note, nesting geese crop tender green shoots amid gravel and brush islands, mallards putter in twosomes, poking among the grass edges of side channels. An occasional blacktail deer will peep from among the poplar and fir trees lining the river.

Tying caddis and other dry flies with blacktail deer hair brings a sense of the river valley to the angler's hand, as well as a bit of practicality. Because blacktail hair is dense and somewhat coarse, with an oily texture, an adaptation to this wet climate, the hair is tough and repels water, an advantage when tying and fishing some deer hair dry flies.

River Dream Time and Gravel Bar Breaks

In our lust for trout we can get caught up in the same hurry and scurry of our everyday lives, whirling down the river, trying to scoop up fish like a trout vacuum cleaner. We yank on waders, string rods and tie flies on tippets with scuffling haste, charging down to the river, then beating the water with a fly rod flail.

Trout lust can blind us to the river and possibly the prime reason we go astream—to get out of the daily grind and into river time, a non-place and non-time removed from familiar reality. We can get so tuned into the hatch or expected hatch and whether the fish will rise, that we don't really see, hear, or smell the river.

If you want to coalesce with the McKenzie, take time out for gravel bars. Sometimes I find the bar well stocked, by reaching into my satchel for a pint of George Dickel or Crown Royal, and a Swisher Sweet Perfecto cigar, but sometimes I don't. Try sitting on a gravel bar with the rod not in hand, just sitting there without casting or searching for rises, but just listening to the river and looking around.

◆

When March Browns are emerging, Soft Hackles are effective, fished both subsurface and in the film.

You may find yourself astride a convenient log, but most likely you'll be at ground level, perched on and among McKenzie River rock. Sure, you may find a heron feather for tying an honest-to-God Spey fly for seducing one of her steelhead, but if you look at the rocks themselves, they tell the true McKenzie River story, a kind of history you can't get by reading a book or looking at pictures. When you pick up a McKenzie River rock you might find one that is smooth, polished by the tumbling of eons of river water. You might handle a bit of volcano, recognized by the pockmarked pores that encased gas pockets within the ejected lava rock that cooled enough for you to handle it thousands of years later.

When you slow down long enough to handle ancient rocks you can hear the river singing to you because you aren't so busy scoping rises or slugging about in loud wading shoes, or thrashing and clanging around in an aluminum drift boat. When you sit down, you slow down.

You are sitting on the McKenzie's history in another sense, too, because during the winter these gravel bar rocks were five feet under water. Instead of being a river fixture, the gravel bar was part of the river's frame, forcing the water ever oceanward. Each gravel bar is a funnel formed by trillions of rocks, some of which you can hold, and by putting a McKenzie rock in your hand, you grip a part of the river.

The Australian aborigines have a kind of dream time where they pass their history down through the generations through cave paintings and rhythmic story telling. You can get into a kind of McKenzie River dream time, letting time and space wash by you, relaxing and flowing with the river. You can touch a bit of volcano on the gravel bar; you can pocket a small rock, taking a bit of the volcano and a bit of the McKenzie with you.

The Western March Brown dun is a particular favorite of dry fly fishermen, matched with a size 12 or 14 light brown Comparadun. Parachutes or traditionals such as the Dark Hendrickson or Dark Cahill also work well.

◆

Summer on the McKenzie

Because of the mild climate in this western part of Oregon, summer just slides in, merging damp May days with brighter June days until average temperatures are in the 70s and the McKenzie hosts the first of the summer hatches. If high water in the spring hasn't knocked them out, you still might encounter fishable hatches of March Browns, and a few McKenzie Caddis in the upper reaches of the river.

One of the first mayflies of early summer hatches is a fluorescent yellow size 14 dun that almost glows in low slanting sun. Interestingly enough, although juvenile fish and sometimes whitefish rise to this bug—which often results in a dampened but still floating insect—adult trout seem to disdain this

◆

When the river isn't high or off-color, the Western March Brown mayfly dun brings fish to the surface. The spinners only occasionally draw trout to the surface.

To get a trout to pounce on your fly, you can dead-drift it or you can make your fly hop an inch or so on the surface like the natural insect.

mayfly. At times I've had good success with a size 14 bright yellow Comparadun on the Santiam River, so maybe others have done well on the McKenzie by matching this hatch.

I've had consistent success matching the more prevalent size 14 and 16 cream mayflies (*Ephemerella, Epeorus, Heptagenia*) with cream Comparaduns, Parachutes, or a favorite traditional, the Light Cahill. The Cahill is excellent for simulating a variety of cream bugs that hatch during the summer; besides the pale mayflies, the Cahill can pass for pale caddis or the Little Yellow stonefly.

My favorite tactic for windy days is dead-drifting a Cahill as you would any dry fly, then either making it hop a bit, or even skittering a Cahill an inch or two, particularly on blustery flats where cutthroat cruise about, searching for insects but not holding in a specific feeding lane.

When fly fishers talk about summer hatches, it's common to hear the "PMD" code word bouncing off the pegboard canyons of fly shops throughout the West, including those that service the McKenzie. The typical Pale Morning Dun (*Ephemerella inermis*) is medium size, a 14 or 16 mayfly with gray wings and pale olive body, but its coloration varies, depending on the river you fish. "PMD" has become a catch-all phrase for a variety of pale mayflies that hatch throughout the West; you'll hear guides and fly shop people talk about the hatch occurring not only in the morning, but in the afternoon on cloudy days or on hot summer evenings. The PMDs on the McKenzie are light brown or creamish-brown, usually close to a size 16. Water and air temperature, as well as water depth and clarity determines the timing of the hatch, which starts in June and continues until it compresses down to the last bit of daylight during the hot weeks of late summer.

Guide Chris Daughters considers the Green Drake mayfly hatch (*Ephemerella doddsi*) underrated by McKenzie anglers, probably because it only lasts a few days. However, when these size 8 mayflies pop, they bring the biggest trout in the river to

"PMD" has become a catch-all phrase for a variety of pale mayflies that hatch throughout the West. The PMDs on the McKenzie are light brown or creamish-brown, usually size 16.

the surface. Because the Green Drake nymph makes its living browsing on the algae covered rocks in the fastest currents, the duns will hatch in the heavy riffles and pocket water. The Green Drake hatches midday, the middle of June, and is matched with a size 8 Wulff style dry, with an olive body, dun hackle, and dark deer hair tail and wings.

An excellent locale to intercept the hatch is on the upper river, and particularly along the McKenzie River National Recreation Trail, which parallels 27 miles of the river. Your best bet is the section from Trail Bridge Reservoir down to the McKenzie Ranger Station, just downstream from Paradise Campground. From Ollalie Campground down is a popular boater's run, and they do well by chucking flies into the pockets and quick runs inaccessible on foot. Check your maps closely because there are access points on the north bank via gravel roads, on the opposite side from the main route, State Highway 126.

One of the first mayflies of early summer hatches as a fluorescent yellow size 12 and 14 dun that almost glows.

McKenzie summer steelhead.

The McKenzie River National Recreation Trail parallels 27 miles of the upper river, designated as the McKenzie Wild and Scenic River Corridor.

The McKenzie River National Recreation Trail offers the chance to hike and fish the river, flicking your fly into trout hidey holes wherever you can get to the river. You will hike and fish among old growth cedar and Douglas fir, occasionally scrambling over fallen tree giants, and negotiating brush and volcanic rock outcroppings. It's a vigorous physical type of fishing; the upper river is robust, a quick flowing, tumbling gush of water, turquoise blue-green from its heritage of volcanic filtering. Upstream from Paradise Campground the river is not

Denise Trowbridge fishes the McKenzie along the National Recreation Trail, flicking her fly into trout hidey holes.

stocked; native rainbow will run up to 14 inches, catch-and-release, barbless hook flies and lures only.

On one fall trip, my 75 year old fishing partner, Don McNeil, came rushing up out of the timber, swatting at himself with his hat, peeling off his jacket and yelling for my help. He had inadvertently stumbled into a yellow jacket wasp nest and they had responded by attacking him. Fortunately, it was a cool fall day and the wasps were somewhat lethargic, with most of them just hanging on to his clothes and not swarming his face. We brushed him down and went looking for a friendlier fishing spot.

There are several other old growth hikes along the upper McKenzie. A good starting place is Delta Campground, halfway between the towns of Blue River and Rainbow. The Delta Old

Lupins along the McKenzie River.

Photo by Virginia Trump.

Growth Grove trail will take you through an amazing one-half mile trek through a cathedral of ancient giants. The road that crosses the McKenzie at Delta Campground is one end of Aufderheide National Scenic Byway, a gorgeous drive along the South Fork of the McKenzie, up past its headwaters to the headwaters of the North Fork of the Middle Fork of the Willamette River. There are Old growth Groves in the French Pete, Skookum Creek, and Fisher Creek areas. The South Fork of the McKenzie has native fish in it, but above Cougar Reservoir is managed as a hatchery stocked stream.

From the town of Blue River you can go north on USFS road 15 to H.J. Andrews Experimental Forest, then turn right on road 1506, go 10 miles to the trailhead of the Lookout Creek Old Growth Trail. The Blue River may look enticing, but I doubt if many fish are in residence since the Army Corps of Engineers drained it in the summer of 1994.

From mid-May on through the fall there is always some type of caddis flitting about on the McKenzie, varying in size from a 14 down to sizes in the 20s. These consistent caddis hatching and egg-laying operations keep McKenzie fish tuned in; it certainly makes sense to use caddis patterns. The standard dry flies work, such as the Elk Hair Caddis, Henryville Special, and for selective trout on the flats, a tent-wing style such as the King's River Caddis. The LaFontaine Emergent Sparkle Pupa in sizes 14 through 20 in cream, tan, or grayish olive, depending on the hatch, will trick many trout for you.

Chris Daughters introduced me to a C-D-C Caddis, tied like an Elk Hair Caddis, but with gray C-D-C hackle substituted for the standard rooster chicken hackle palmered along the body. The tendrils of the C-D-C hackle trail back, looking very bug-like. Don't add floatant, it will clog up the C-D-C fibers, causing the fly to sink. A crisp backcast will dry the fly.

A predominant hatch in July are the Little Yellow stoneflies (*Isoperla, Isogenus*), a slender size 14 stonefly with a bright yellow body and creamy yellow wings and legs. These slim stoneflies hatch mid-stream and in the shallows from midday on towards evening. The returning females lay their eggs in the same time frame, causing trout to feed with gusto.

In *Western Hatches*, authors Rick Hafele and Dave Hughes write that these lean nymphs are predatory, and they "are especially active, crawling quickly along the bottom. They are frequently dislodged from the bottom and drift in the current. When dislodged, they swim with a side-to-side, snake-like wiggle. Their swimming is feeble, but unusual among the stoneflies. During their pre-emergence migrations from fast riffles to slow shallows more nymphs are dislodged." You can match the nymph with a size 14, 2X-long tan Hare's Ear, either dead-drifted or animated with some line tension in fast current or fished more actively with a hand-twist retrieve in slow water.

Bob Guard of the Caddisfly says, "I've had some of my best fishing during the Little Yellow stonefly hatch with a Wet Cahill, size 14 to 18, fished as an emerger. I'll quarter my cast downstream and let it fish across in the classic wet fly style. I'll fish the Wet Cahill until the hatch is really coming off, then I'll switch to a dry. During the emergence I've taken rainbows up to just a hair over 19 inches on the McKenzie with a Wet Cahill. Twice I've hooked summer-run steelhead during the Little Yellow stonefly hatch but I landed neither of them."

You can use a yellow Elk Hair Caddis for the adult, or tie the specific imitation in yellow with an optional short deer hair tail, dubbed body, deer hair wing and cream hackle. Some like to include a bright red butt to imitate the females' egg sac. I tie some with cream C-D-C hackle up front. Cartoonist Gene Trump had trouble tracking the flush-film version of the dry,

Chris Daughters introduced me to the CDC Caddis.

From mid-May through the fall there is always some type of caddis flittering about on the McKenzie, varying in size from a 14 down to a size 20.

particularly in the fading light of evening, so he substitutes a white calf tail wing for better visibility. Be sure to carry a few stonefly patterns with you when on the river in the summer, because at times the hatch is heavy and trout become very selective to the Little Yellow stoneflies.

A cream Soft Hackle is also an excellent summer fly for the McKenzie, standing in for a variety of aquatic insects, including cream mayflies, caddis and stoneflies. Keep it simple, with a slender tan or cream dubbed body, ribbed with thin gold wire, and two turns of tan grouse, partridge or hen chicken. You can vary your tactics to fish this Soft Hackle deeply sunken as a nymph, or just under the surface, or awash in the surface film as an emerger or spent adult. Optionally, you can use "raw" undyed duck flank feathers for the front hackle; the natural oil in the feather will keep the fly in the surface film.

McKenzie trout are not strange and bizarre creatures that require a size 32 Kliptonator fly tied under a full moon and dipped in bat sweat. Boaters that pound the bank with an attractor pattern such as a size 12 Royal Wulff will garner strikes. For wading anglers, normal trout tactics for working a nymph, dry, or emerger will be successful on the McKenzie. As I've mentioned, I find the traditional Light Cahill effective, as well as the Adams. Standard western patterns such as the Elk Hair Caddis and Humpy work, too, particularly as high floaters in rough, rowdy water. But I've discovered that in many places where I fish for trout, including the McKenzie, the qualities that make these flies high floaters may actually diminish their effectiveness, especially in calmer waters.

My approach is to reduce the hair and hackle, presenting the fish with a cleaner outline and a fly that floats more in the film, where the fish can see it, than floating above the water. Because the hackle barbules tend to keep the hook from penetrating the fish's mouth, reduced hackle means more hook-ups.

I've done well on the McKenzie with a Reduced Humpy in cream in sizes 14 and 16, possibly because it simulates a cream caddis, mayfly or Little Yellow stone perhaps emerging and stuck in its nymphal case. The Reduced Caddis is a trimmed

Wild cutthroat trout predominate in the lower part of the river.

down Elk Hair Caddis, simply a dubbed body with a deer hair wing and no hackle. The Reduced Caddis floats in the film, just like a caddis stuck on the water, unable to fly. It's especially effective in tan, cream, and dark brown in sizes 16 to 20. I've seldom seen trout on the McKenzie rise to midges, but the trout cruising the high lakes in the upper watershed feed heavily on midges, well matched by a reduced Griffith's Gnat. After tying the Gnat with peacock body, fine wire and palmered griz-

Be sure to carry some little yellow stonefly patterns with you when on the river this summer.

zly hackle, trim the hackle top and bottom, leaving only the side hackle. The fly then floats flush, just like an emerging midge. When there is no predominant hatch and the fish won't respond to attractor patterns, but I want a fly with a white wing for better visibility, I'll go with a Royal Coachman Trude in size 16. Packing the same coloration as the Royal Wulff, this Trude mimics a lot of bugs, including terrestrials, in a general sort of way. I carry both reduced and full versions of standard patterns for flats and riffles, and often switch back and forth in a day's fishing.

As the light wanes at dusk on the hot evenings of late July and August, you may see Gene Trump with a crazed look in his eye, trying to dupe hard-to-catch redsides that cruise right in close to shore. These are fat, husky trout that are wary of thick tippets, flies larger than a size 18, and sloppy presentations. With a size 18 or 20 red Humpy or his Reduced Parachute Adams, Gene makes careful casts with a long leader and slender tippet. The Reduced Adams version consists of a black thread body, white poly post-wing and grizzly hackle. The hackle fibers that radiate from around the post-wing also simulate a tail. But he doesn't always catch those challenging trout, hence the crazed eyes.

The McKenzie is extremely popular with boaters and rafters; boaters work the March Brown and McKenzie caddis hatch in the spring, and the upper river is particularly popular with summer rafters. To escape your fellow fisher persons in the summer, try fishing the last little bit of daylight or the first

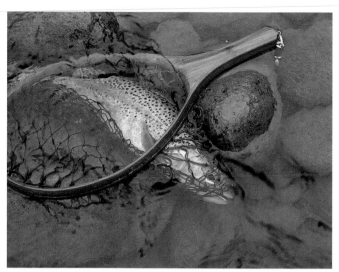

Normal trout tactics for working a nymph, dry, or emerger will be successful on the McKenzie.

◆

morning hours. You may encounter a few duns hatching in the morning, but you're more likely to find trout feeding on spinners of the mayflies that hatched the previous evenings, and on emerging caddis or the spent caddis adults. Although hoppers rarely find themselves on the river, McKenzie trout take waterborne terrestrials on summer mornings, making generalist patterns such as a reduced Humpy or Royal Trude effective.

In any case, you'll need caution when stalking rising trout because these fish have been cast to all year, and trout tend to be more wary on clear summer mornings. Crouch low, wade slowly and quietly, creep up on your fish, cast sidearm if possible, and keep your line, leader and tippet upstream of the fish so as to not line the fish. When walking the bank, searching for risers, be alert for subtle rises; morning rising trout will feed with soft sips, just barely creasing the skin of the river.

The returning McKenzie summer steelhead assumes a trout-like quality, and in fact, many steelhead are hooked by trouters who usually lose the fish because of a trout-rated tippet. The first summer runs will show in June, but the majority of the fish arrive in the late summer and into fall. You will often find steelhead in the tailouts in early morning. You can get these fish to take your fly, providing you can present your fly without spooking your quarry. Once again, wade cautiously and quietly, keep low, cast low if possible, and swing your fly in front of the fish without spooking it. Because you won't be able to see the fish once you start your stalk, you simply work your fly and hope you haven't scared the fish. Some favorite patterns are size 6 and 8 Purple Peril, Green Butt Skunk and other dark toned, slender steelhead flies. I like to use my McKenzie Spey because I tie it with heron feathers I find along the river; you may enjoy developing your own particular pattern for the McKenzie steelhead. There aren't a lot of steelhead in the river this time of year, but certainly enough to fish for, and it's a delight to be astream of a summer morning. And you may witness another hunter that frequents the early morning McKenzie, the bald eagle.

When water and air temperatures rise in August, hatches are slight and compressed into the last minutes of daylight. If you can get out on the river during the coolness of the occasional rainstorm, you may encounter increased bug activity which triggers renewed trout feeding. However, during the dead of summer you might consider some alternatives to fishing the main river, such as in the high country. Trail Bridge Reservoir and Carmen Reservoir on the upper river exhibit cool water temperatures even when it's in the 90s in the valley. I prefer Carmen because of its extensive weed beds (which harbor lots of aquatic insects for trout to eat) and because it's a couple of miles off the main highway. Most summer evenings will find bugs hatching and trout rising and few, if any, fishermen. The best way to fish is via a floating craft, and a float tube is ideal, although you'll need neoprene waders for the cold water.

The main highway, 126, shadows the upper river from Trail Bridge Reservoir downstream, but the McKenzie "disappears" between Carmen and Trail Bridge. From Carmen, part is siphoned underground to Smith Reservoir and then through a tunnel to Trail Bridge, and part just dribbles downhill to disappear in a vast lava field.

From Carmen upstream to Clear Lake, the McKenzie is a "river without seasons" because the banks are lush with greenery year-round, watered by heavy mist wafting from the river as it crashes down through a cramped canyon carved through ancient volcanic tubes. A few hardy, small trout live in this stretch, but it's arduous fishing. I prefer to hike this section,

◆

Denise Trowbridge with an average size McKenzie River trout.

Photo by Brian O'Keefe

The McKenzie is extremely popular with boaters and rafters.

◆

admiring its beauty without torturing myself trying to negotiate the steep cliffs, fallen timber and heavy brush. Massive old growth Douglas fir and cedar cast muted shadows in a interplay of sun and silhouette in a cathedral of light. The McKenzie rushes and roars, blue-green in the sunlight, darker in shade, but not contained or tamed, a vigorous outpouring of the bloodstream of life on this planet—water in its purest form. The McKenzie leaps from Koosah and Sahalie Falls, spring boarding

───────────◆───────────

When fishing slows on the main river, you might consider the joys of fishing the high mountain lakes that form part of the headwater system of the McKenzie.

into space, spraying mist that forms rainbows in the sun while watering the dense moss and fern covered rock bulwarks of the river canyon. The counterpoint between the blue-green rushing river and dense greenery sends tendrils of soothing renewal into a fisherman's soul; it's a primal touchstone for the urban seeker.

Many consider Clear Lake as the head of the McKenzie, although strictly speaking, the water percolating out from the vast lava fields north of Fish Lake supplies the true genesis of the river. Fish Lake feeds Fish Lake Creek which trickles into Clear Lake. (By late summer Fish Lake is too shallow to fish.) However, Clear Lake is gorgeous, created by a lava dam that backed up 148 acres of super clear water to a depth of 175 feet, and as such sets the character for the whole McKenzie system. Geologically, Clear Lake is new; only 3,000 years ago Little Nash Crater erupted, spilling lava to form the dam that created Clear Lake, inundating many trees which you can still see upright on the bottom of the lake. These botanical fossils haven't decomposed because the water in Clear averages less than 40 degrees year-round.

Because of Clear Lake's super clear water, from shore a float tuber looks to be suspended, not attached to water or land, but dangling in time and space. That extreme water clarity means spooky fish that can be tough to catch. The rainbow and brook trout also learn to be wary of hunting osprey, who spy fish easily in the transparent water. You'll do best early, when the fish feed in the shaded areas along the shore, and late in the day, and when it's cloudy and breezy enough to mask your presentation. Rental rowboats are available at the north end of the lake, but no motors are allowed, to maintain water purity.

When fishing slows on the main river, you might consider the joys of fishing the high mountain lakes that form part of the headwater system of the McKenzie. Because I fear there is a danger of over-exposing any particular high mountain lake in the Cascades because they are so small, instead of mentioning any specific lakes, I'm going to describe the fishing you might expect, and point you in the right direction so you can find a bit of fishing adventure on your own.

Get a Willamette National Forest map and a Three Sisters Wilderness Area map from the sources listed at the back, then plan your outing. If you like to backpack, then you can expand your fishing territory, particularly if you strap a float tube onto your pack. Lakes near the road will be fished hardest; the farther you walk, the better the fishing, and a mile will eliminate 90% of the anglers. If you don't backpack in and stay overnight, you might use a National Forest Campground as your base, and day hike to a fishing spot. You can use a variety of floating crafts; my preference is for the open bow float tubes that have high tech plastic bladders and valves that allow you to inflate them with a raft-type foot or hand pump once you get to the lake. (Some manufacturers offer a replacement bladder for old style round tubes equipped with rubber tire inner tubes.)

You'll hike through quiet glens of Douglas fir, hemlock, cedar, rhododendron, sword fern, beargrass, spring-blooming trillium, and dwarf Oregon grape, framed by outcroppings of moss encrusted volcanic rock. I love being in the high country, feasting on the sights and smells, but I have to admit that I hate the hard work of the climb. It is this essence of manual labor

The McKenzie leaps from Sahalie Falls, spraying mist and watering the dense moss and ferns that cover the rock bulwarks of the river canyon.

♦

that separates out the teeming masses from the wilderness elevations. A backpacker leaves behind all the non-essentials: the excess weight of modern conveniences, the urban roar and smoke of daily life, and the elbow jostle of fellow men and women. You abandon the hectic rhythms of every day exis-

♦

When water and air temperatures rise in August, hatches are slight and compressed into the last minutes of daylight.

Standing above Sahalie Falls, you can see how the McKenzie rushes and roars.

tence in exchange for simplistic eating, resting, sleeping and fishing, all to the welcome sound of silence—few people, if any, no motors or vehicles of any kind, even mountain bikes—just the calls of ravens and Clark's nutcrackers or the quick splash of a feeding trout. Sweat from physical exercise is the coin of the realm, and even though our wilderness areas are open to all, relatively few are willing to pay the admission price.

I wouldn't say that high lakes are hard to fish, but why is it that alpine lakes are invariably brushy, too boggy to wade, and generally tree-lined? Without a float tube, catching fish is only part of the challenge—the first step is getting the fly out to the fish as they cruise by just out of casting range, sipping insects only a few feet past your best cast. But to the tuber, the whole lake is readily accessible, no matter where the trout are feeding. Backpacking the additional weight of a float tube and fins is extra work, but the payoff is silent stalking and effortless casting to cruising mountain trout.

In the high altitude the sun warms both terrestrial and aquatic insects quickly. Trout respond by easing into the shallows to browse near submerged vegetation and off ledges and snags, dining on midge pupae, damselfly and dragonfly nymphs, *Callibaetis* mayflies, and terrestrials such as ants and beetles.

Enter the float tuber. Donning waders and flippers, the tuber slips into the floating easy chair, eases out from shore, and fins out to the deeper water adjacent to the feeding grounds that circle the lake like a fascinating doughnut of piscine activity. Casts are snicked into the shallows with only thin air to caress the backcast.

With a little plop the forward cast drops the lightly weighted size 16 *Callibaetis* nymph only a few feet from shore, but in the danger zone of feeding brook trout. The hand-twist retrieve is begun with tense fingers, anticipating the strike. The gentle nudge on the nymph is answered with an upraised rod and a tight line hung to an enraged trout streaking for deeper water.

Because of Clear Lake's super clear water, from shore a float tuber looks to be suspended.

The light rod bows double, snubbing the trout short of freedom. The 10-inch brookie reluctantly gives watery ground, splashing furiously on the surface.

The sweat and work of backpacking a float tube is rewarded with unique fishing—effortless floating from a comfortable chair without a care in the world while casting to cruising trout in a crystalline alpine lake.

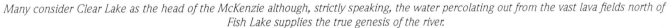

Many consider Clear Lake as the head of the McKenzie although, strictly speaking, the water percolating out from the vast lava fields north of Fish Lake supplies the true genesis of the river.

The first major hatch of the late season is the fall caddis, a size 8 rusty orange caddis that provokes the larger redsides to the top, especially on overcast days.

◆

Fall on the McKenzie

Although the calendar may indicate that fall is here, the first of September finds the McKenzie Valley still wrapped in summer's clutches, with warm nights and hot days, which continue until the first cooling autumnal rains hit around the third week in September.

These rains are part of the Indian summer that will continue on until mid-October when heavy rains can knock the river out of shape. However, in many years the rains only signal the fall fishing for restless steelhead and casting to trout rising to hatches of the little Blue Wing Olive mayflies. The best part of the fall fishing is after the first cooling rains, but before the heavy November deluges that knock the river out.

The first major hatch of the late season is the Fall Caddis (Limnephilidae: Dicosmoecus), a size 8 rusty orange caddis that provokes the larger redsides to the top, especially on overcast days. Other common names for this jumbo caddis are the Orange Sedge or October Caddis. However, on the upper McKenzie this caddis begins hatching during the first part of September. Various dry fly patterns simulate this bulky bug, such as the Bucktail Caddis or an orange Stimulator. My choice is the Madam X tied with a tuft of fluorescent green or orange yarn on top of the wing for better visibility in the low light of canyon shade or under drooping trees that stretch fly-snatching fingers out over the river. Sometimes smaller fish will chase your caddis imitation, but I've had my best luck, particularly with the bigger fish, when the fly is dead-drifted through the run. With the low light of evening, redsides and husky cut-

throat will ease into the shallow riffles to feed, but most of your action will be in the long, fairly deep runs where the bigger trout have stationed themselves during the higher water temperatures of summer. And often the best spot is the one that is the most difficult to cast to or get at with a dead-drift, because that is the spot where most people don't present their fly—a safety space for trout.

At the other extreme, you can have excellent and challenging dry fly fishing when you get a "*Baetis* Day", an overcast, calm, fall day with maybe a slight sporadic rain or light mist. The little Blue Wing Olive mayflies hatch in size 18 or 20, drifting steadily down those same deep slow runs where the bigger trout have stationed themselves. Dorsaling, porpoising rises that signal steady feeding by big trout on small insects will signal you to slip a size 18 or 20 Adams, Parachute Adams, Comparadun, or emerger in a dead-drift over these fish. But beware, after a season of being flogged by fly fishers, these trout are extremely wary and easily put down. Go with a fine tippet without lining the fish, presenting the fly first to fool these fish.

You may enjoy equally pleasant days astream when a sprinkling of various insects are hatching or laying eggs. When these dancing bugs alert trout to top-water feeding, but there is no predominant hatch, I've had good luck with a size 14 or 16 Royal Wulff, which is particularly effective on overcast days because I can see those white wings, and maybe the fish can too. On clear fall days when the sunlight slants low across the river, I've done well with a size 14, 16 or 18 Yellow Humpy,

◆

The Royal Wulff in size 14 or 16 can be an effective fly in the fall, and the white wings make the floating fly easy to see.

Goodpasture Bridge, built in 1938, is the second longest covered bridge in Oregon.

and especially a Reduced Humpy with pale deer hair wing and tail, cream dubbed body and one brown or grizzly hackle. The light tan deer hair wing "lights up" in that low angle sunlight; again, I can see it clearly and I believe the trout can, too.

You might bear in mind that a modest run of Chinook salmon glides upriver about mid-September. These fish have traveled some 200 miles in freshwater, and as such are not bright fish and should be allowed to spawn without harassment from fly fishermen. However, trout don't overlook the fact that while spawning, some salmon eggs drift loose in the current, offering a tasty snack for rainbow and cutthroat holding just downstream. With micro eggs and a weight on the leader you can catch trout by easing your fake egg downstream from the salmon without disturbing their spawning.

Fall Steelheading

The McKenzie summer steelhead are Skamania stock hatchery fish raised at the facility at Leaburg. The run is sustained by a yearly release of 108,000 adipose-fin-clipped smolts. The adult steelhead return averages from 2,000 to 3,000 fish. Most have spent two years feeding in the ocean, returning at a weight of seven to nine pounds; a few will spend three years at sea, returning in the 12- to 13-pound class. Of the 400 to 1,000 fish that spawn upstream from Leaburg dam, 10% are non-fin-clipped adults. (Biologists get fairly accurate data from video tape of fish ascending the dam).

Because of their origin at the hatchery at Leaburg Dam, most of the adults will hang around the water at the dam and downstream for a few miles. There is public access at the hatchery at Leaburg Dam. The hatchery parking lot is on the south side of the river, reached by driving across Leaburg Dam, about five miles upstream from the town of Leaburg. (This is not fly-angling-only water; you'll be in the company of conventional steelheaders using lures and bait.)

By the time these adult fish swim back up the Columbia, up the Willamette, and finally up the McKenzie, they take on

Long rodders seeking steelhead use traditional wet flies such as the Lady Caroline in the classic wet fly swing, while others use dry fly skaters to bring steelies to the top.

Photo by Gene Trump

Although probably not as durable as an aluminum or fiberglass boat, the classic wooden drift boat (which some say originated on the McKenzie) opens up water that wading fishermen can't reach.

◆

many of the characteristics of giant trout. They rest in tailouts, in deep runs, and in riffles. And sometimes they take trout flies such as nymphs, or dries such as Elk Hair Caddis, which can be very exciting, but landing an eight-pound sea-run trout on a light tippet can be tough. Long rodders seeking steelhead use traditional flies such as the Green Butt Skunk or Purple Peril in the classic wet fly swing, while others use dry fly skaters to bring steelies to the top.

Allan Cline of the Homewaters Fly Shop loves to entice steelhead to the surface, especially from mid-September through October, and even into November during low water years. He uses a 9-1/2-foot rod with an eight weight line. He prefers a light colored fly line so he can easily track it, but he dyes the last 30 feet of line with Rit seafoam green dye so as to not spook the fish. He runs a 12-foot leader with 8-pound Maxima Ultragreen as the tippet.

He says, "I don't think the fly pattern makes that much difference". He uses a size 6 or size 4 Muddler or a Cline's Steelhead Caddis, which has a spun deer hair head and either a yellow or orange foam body.

"I'll cast either across the stream or quartering downstream, depending on the current. If it's slower, I'll cast across the stream and even let a little belly into the fly line. I will put a pop on it every so often, almost like you'd work a bass popper. Put a little twitch to it. But normally, I'm trying to make that fly tease, as slowly as possible, where it's waking. I don't want it swinging fast; I want it to dangle over particular spots and I'll do whatever mending is necessary to keep the fly waking, but tracking as slowly as possible."

If a steelhead boils the dry and won't take it, or if a fish misses the dry and doesn't feel the hook, Cline will come back with a Skunk or Green Butt Skunk, size 4 or 6.

Cline prefers to fish from an anchored boat, and applies a riffle hitch to his fly to increase its effectiveness. Instead of riffle hitching the fly to the right or the left, as you would fishing from shore, he puts one hitch behind the head of the fly so the tippet comes out right under the fly, centered on the hook shank.

Possibly just as important is the type of water Cline fishes: "I particularly like tailouts and runs for dry fly fishing, and the sides of runs and tailouts. If other boats have been through, a lot of times the fish will move off the tailouts and will tuck into the first rocks on either side of it, sometimes in quite shallow water. I usually fish dry flies from a boat, and I'll work the water to either side and down. I'll drop down 30 feet or so and I'll work it again.

"I work down on the tailouts and I'll also work the runs. If it's a good rocky run with plenty of cover where I know steelhead hold, I'll work that pretty well. There are certain spots that you learn, and you tend to fish them over and over again. You learn where the fish hold in these runs and so you work those areas pretty hard. When you first start out, you just have to go by guess and what looks like good steelhead water. You probe it, and then as you start getting fish, you go back to those areas."

While it's true you'll probably catch more McKenzie steelhead in the fall by swinging the infamous Green Butt Skunk in the classic wet fly style, you'll never forget that steelhead taking your dry in a big boil or an open-mouthed pounce. Your memory will be forever burned by that dark head, white inner mouth and rainbow stripe of the full-body lunge of a steelhead taking your dry.

◆

Jimson grows in gravel patches along the river, flowering in the fall.

November

November 1st marks an important change in available fishing waters on the McKenzie: the river is only open from Leaburg Dam downstream. You can fly fish for steelhead and whitefish from there down to Hayden Bridge; from Hayden to the mouth, it's open for steelhead, whitefish, and catch-and-release trout fishing.

Some years the weather remains mild until mid-November, but in normal years the McKenzie is belted with heavy rains in late October that bulge the river to its bankside trees, turning the river into a chocolate highway of floating brush and debris. Eventually the river clears, but water temperatures drop to the 40s and the fishing complexion of the river changes. (If you're looking for clear water to fish, check out the river closer to Leaburg; Mohawk River tends to contribute turbidity to the lower river, just downstream from Hayden Bridge.)

You can check the river level by calling the National Oceanic and Atmospheric Administration in Eugene at (541) 688-9041 for a local weather recording that allows you to eventually speak to a weather person who can give you the river reading at Vida. Generally, the river fishes well when the reading is two feet or below (At 1.9 feet the river flow at Vida is 3,000 cfs).

Some misty November days host little Blue Wing Olive mayfly hatches and rising fish, but most often it's a nymphing affair. And even when the Baetis are hatching, the trout and whitefish may not get into rising. Water clarity, river height and water temperatures all play a role, not to mention the indecipherable disposition of the fish that might make them ignore a perfectly good hatch.

I love steelheading during those misty fall days when the last of the golden leaves shine in the intermittent sun. You can catch fish with the floating line and the classic wet fly swing or grease lining or using a sinktip and swinging the wet fly low. But I've had my best success with a bright fluorescent floating

Jay Collins battles a McKenzie summer-run steelhead.

line, long leader, small bright fly, dead-drifted fairly close to the bottom via split shot. You catch fish that stop the fly much like a jumbo trout taking a nymph, and I've had steelhead nail the fly as it starts to slowly bend its way back to me, much like a deeply sunken wet fly.

I find the nymphing technique is the most effective strategy when the river conditions are less than ideal, when November and December storms bring cold rain, dropping water temperatures into the low 40s, causing steelhead to hug the bottom of the river. There is no glamour in pitching a fly and split shot, but there are many days when the steelhead just won't move to a fly unless it drifts right up to them; on those days a nymph-style presentation is best for catching steelhead. And, as I've mentioned, because McKenzie steelhead have migrated so far, they seem to exhibit pronounced trout-like characteristics. They take your steelhead fly on the dead-drift much like a trout taking a large nymph.

There are unlimited variations to the basic theme of a compact, bright fly. A favorite of mine is the Caballero, with a body of fluorescent green chenille and fluorescent red or pink chenille and fluorescent red or pink hackle. Optional dressings abound, including adding a tail or some sparkle material for a wing. I tie it on a standard black steelhead streamer hook or a short shank hook. For nymphing presentations, a Gamakatsu Octopus hook reduces snag-ups because of its curved, offset bend, and it fishes well because the steel is hard and the point is very sharp.

Although you can catch steelhead on foot, you can cover more water and up your chances considerably by using a boat to get you to wade-able water or by positioning the boat so you

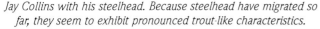

Jay Collins with his steelhead. Because steelhead have migrated so far, they seem to exhibit pronounced trout-like characteristics.

Some misty November days host little Blue Wing Olive mayfly hatches and rising fish, but most often it's a nymphing affair.

can cast to holding water. And whether on foot or casting from a boat, winter days are so short that you want to concentrate your efforts on what I think of as high-percentage waters: in riffles, along the edge of the main current in runs and tailouts, along ledges, behind rocks or in any area where steelhead can hold with minimum effort.

You can use a 7 through 9 weight rod, depending on what you find comfortable to cast, but don't overlook Spey rods. These 13 to 15 foot rods are ideal for controlling the line and the fly's drift, particularly when the holding water is out a little ways from where you can wade. A Spey rod is dandy out of a boat, too, because you can keep the fly well away from the boat and your partner, and yet successfully cover lots of water. And because you are using your shoulder and back muscles instead of using just the wrist and forearm of your casting arm, and because you can cast with either side of your body, I find a two-hand Spey rod less tiring over a day's fishing.

One chilly November day Chris Daughters and I floated the McKenzie for steelhead; the water temperature was 45 degrees, air temperature 41 degrees, river level at Vida 1.7 feet and jade green, commonly known as steelhead green. Gray, wet clouds used my raincoat hood for a skid plate as a storm surged in from the Pacific. A typical November day on the McKenzie. In the first heavy riffle we fished, we had anchored off to the side, so I pitched the fluorescent floating line, long leader, small bright fly, and enough split shot to get a good drift. I had great control because of the Spey rod's 14-foot length, and could easily mend the line, steering the nymph down the chute. I saw the tip of the line hesitate and begin curling upstream, so I set the hook but I missed the take.

We then proceeded farther downstream, landing at an island. Chris fished the tailout and riffle of the main run, while I switched to a 9-1/2-foot rod with a floating 7 weight to try a side channel. I swung a Caballero cross current, wet fly style, without success. Before leaving, I went back through with a small shot on the tippet, just enough weight so the fly would swing lower and slower in front of the fish. A seven pound male rapped the fly and hooked himself on the tight line. He crashed and thrashed around in the run, but eventually fatigued and I brought him to hand.

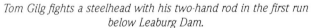

Tom Gilg fights a steelhead with his two-hand rod in the first run below Leaburg Dam.

Tom Gilg with his steelhead. When steelheading the McKenzie, don't overlook Spey rods. These 13 to 15 foot rods are ideal for controlling the line and the fly's drift.

We remounted the boat and fished our way downstream. I kept encouraging Chris to try my Spey rod, particularly since I knew he had experience casting Spey rods. Also, since I had already nailed a fish, I wanted him to get one.

I had gone to my change-up fly, which I do when I either grow tired of using a small bright fly or I figure I'll just rile the fish with something outrageous. My Marabou Flash has a bright red poly flash body, red marabou tail, and individual clumps of marabou for a matuka-style wing, of pink, red and purple, interspersed with fluorescent blue Flashabou and pearl Crystal Flash, tied on a 2/0 hook. This particular run was deep, so I had strapped on three heavy shot; my intention was to dead-drift the fly, allowing all that marabou and flash to attract fish, and then swing the fly cross-current, in a deep wet fly swing designed to tantalize and infuriate territorial steelhead.

Eventually we came to water that was tame enough for Chris to allow me to man the oars. Chris pitched out the fly and was amazed at how much water he could cover and how much control he had over the fly's drift. As I eased us down the run, he made a cast that dropped the fly into the downstream flow below a giant submerged boulder. The fly drifted three feet, the bright fly line bent upstream, and Chris set the hook.

As the long Spey rod bent, Chris said, "I think I'm hung up."

He reefed a little more on the rod, and then the rod bucked as his eight-pound snag came unglued. The furious steelhead plunged downstream, fighting deep in the heavy run. I stroked

Leaburg Dam.

the oars, gliding the drift boat up on a sandy beach, partly because it was an excellent place to land the boat, but also because you need extra room to land fish on a Spey rod.

Even when we could see that the fish wouldn't set any world records, Chris exclaimed how much bigger the fish felt on the longer rod. (The fish has a longer lever on you, too; the fish exerts more pressure on you, making it seem like a larger fish.) Chris fought the fish until it tired, then swung it ashore and tailed it. (You can't land steelhead close to you, as you would with a 9-foot rod, because the 14-foot rod executes a scissoring movement: the tip springs to the side, scooting your fish out of reach. You have to beach it or a companion has to grab it for you.)

I'm certainly not saying that this is the only way to fly fish for steelhead, but I've found that these longer rods have certainly opened up additional water for me, including spots where you can only roll cast. Those long rods do an excellent job of roll casting. In addition, Spey rods are a joy for working a floating line with dries, greased lining, or classic wet fly tactics.

The McKenzie is certainly not a world class steelhead fishery, and it's certain that you won't always catch steelhead on the McKenzie. But if you do go out on the river, you'll raise your odds of catching a fish considerably more than your zero chances if you stay home.

◆

The McKenzie is not a world class steelhead fishery, and you won't always catch steelhead on it.

McKenzie trout don't overlook the fact that mountain whitefish spawn in December.

December—A Year's End

When the carousel of the seasons rotates to December, the fly fishing gypsy must steal moments suitable for the long rod. If the weather is mild and the river is low and clear, you might find enough Baetis hatching to coax some trout to the rise. You'll catch more trout subsurface, fooling trout with nymphs that resemble what trout eat to sustain themselves, such as with a Hare's Ear or Pheasant Tail.

This time of year McKenzie trout don't overlook the fact that Mountain whitefish or Rocky Mountain whitefish (*Prosopium williamsoni*) spawn in December. When trout spawn, they build a nest among small well aerated rocks on the river bottom; whitefish simply broadcast their eggs, allowing the eggs to cling to the rocks via a sticky mucous that covers the eggs.

Some eggs don't adhere to the bottom, but drift free in the current, offering a ready meal for hungry trout. Also, while trout spawn primarily in riffles, whitefish spawn in gravel flats and tailouts, as well as riffles, which expands the trout egg-feeding territory.

Although whitefish eggs are a pale translucent golden color and measure a little over 1mm in diameter, I've had excellent success with pink or red yarn eggs 5 and 7mm in diameter. Because they reduce snag-ups but still hook fish well, I prefer extra-short humped-shank hooks marketed as caddis larva, shrimp or grub hooks, such as the Tiemco 2487 or the Daiichi 1130. The 2X-heavy wire of the Tiemco 2457 is an advantage

when fishing rivers such as the McKenzie, where you might hook a steelhead. You can make a yarn egg imitation by simply super gluing a pre-formed yarn ball to the hook. Use Zap-A-Gap super glue or other cyanoacrylate glue designed to fill in gaps between the bonded materials. Pre-formed yarn balls are marketed under names such as Pom-Poms or Puffy Poms, found in the craft or notions department.

The yarn-egg nymphing strategy is simple: dead-drift your yarn egg fairly close to the bottom, striking when you detect a fish taking the fly. Since these little bits of yarn formed into an egg shape are neutrally buoyant, free-drifting in the current, you must affix lead to the line or leader or add a weighted nymph on a dropper to get the egg down to the fish. The advantage is that you appeal to trout by providing several different food items. The disadvantage is that you tend to snag up more often, and you need to slow your cast and open the casting loop to prevent the flies from tangling.

To better detect the strike you can use an indicator; the most efficient strike indicators are designed so you can move the bobber up or down the line, modifying the placement to best track the egg drifting through varied currents and water depths. When a fish intercepts your nymph or egg, the end of the fly line or your indicator will dip a bit or curl slightly back upstream. By closely watching your line or indicator you can quickly set the hook when a fish takes the egg.

Because of lower water temperatures in December, steelhead hug the bottom and are less likely to move more than a few inches to take your fly. You must irritate the ironhead into

McKenzie River Flies

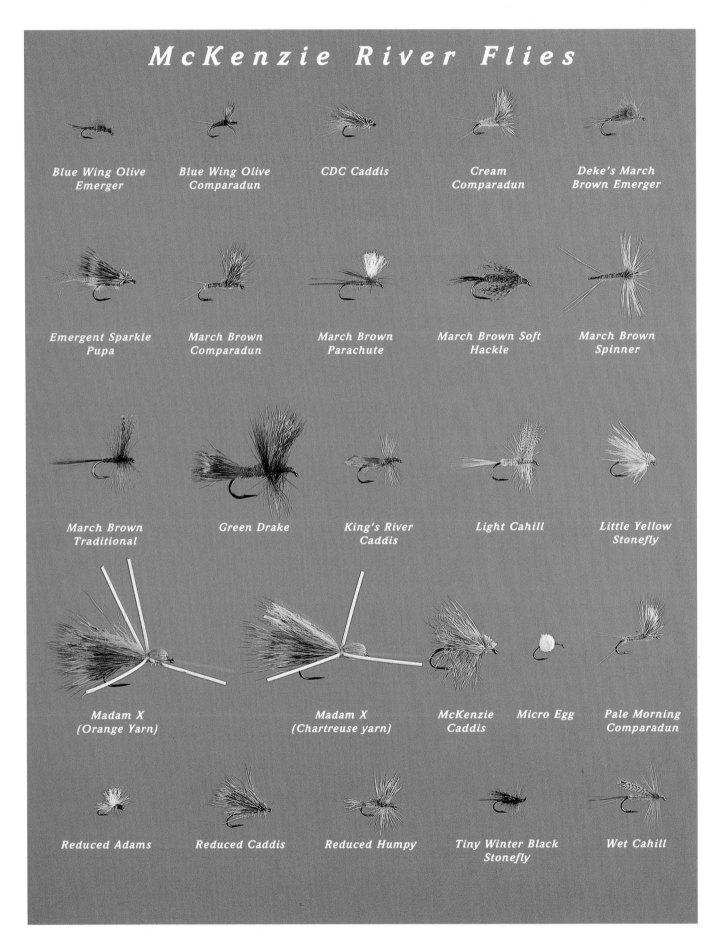

Blue Wing Olive
Emerger

Blue Wing Olive
Comparadun

CDC Caddis

Cream
Comparadun

Deke's March
Brown Emerger

Emergent Sparkle
Pupa

March Brown
Comparadun

March Brown
Parachute

March Brown Soft
Hackle

March Brown
Spinner

March Brown
Traditional

Green Drake

King's River
Caddis

Light Cahill

Little Yellow
Stonefly

Madam X
(Orange Yarn)

Madam X
(Chartreuse yarn)

McKenzie
Caddis

Micro Egg

Pale Morning
Comparadun

Reduced Adams

Reduced Caddis

Reduced Humpy

Tiny Winter Black
Stonefly

Wet Cahill

Steelhead Muddler

Cline's Steelhead
Caddis

Caballero

Marabou Flash

Green Butt Skunk

Purple Peril

McKenzie Spey

Halloween Spey

Deke Meyer with a McKenzie steelhead.

biting your fly by presenting a bright pattern right in front of its nose. It takes faith to be a December McKenzie steelheader.

Some Decembers in the McKenzie valley are mild, resulting in lower than usual water flows, extending the fly fishing season on through the end of the year. Normal Decembers, however, soon bring cold rain or snow, water temperatures drop and the river comes up, limiting the number of fishable days in the month. Nevertheless, you can steal days from daily life, slipping away to the Mother McKenzie to fly fish for an afternoon, even though it's just for a few fleeting hours.

Current and Future Status of McKenzie Steelhead and Trout

Barring some unforeseen eruption of one of the quiet volcanoes in the Cascades that form the wellsprings of the McKenzie, the yearly parade of hatchery steelhead smolts and returning adult steelhead should remain at present levels. The current bag limit of two adult fin-clipped fish over 20 inches per day, not more than six fish in seven consecutive days should remain the same.

Hatchery steelhead returning to the Leaburg facility can actually swim up into holding pond number 6, where the public can view these fish. Fish not used for spawning purposes are trucked downstream and re-released into the McKenzie, offering anglers another shot at them. Hatchery personnel use a dart gun to imbed a Floy anchor tag, a nylon "T-bar", in the base of the dorsal fin, to mark re-released steelhead so they are not counted twice at the hatchery.

Biologists don't need those tags returned because those tags don't give any needed information (except to tell the hatchery that the fish has been counted). However, if you regularly catch McKenzie steelhead and keep some sort of log, biologists are keenly interested in knowing how many of the steelhead you catch are tagged. That kind of information will help contribute to steelhead population estimates of fish caught below Leaburg. (Because of the Leaburg dam viewing station and video taping, biologists have good data on upstream steelhead.)

Currently, over 100,000 fin-clipped hatchery catchable rainbow are planted in the mainstem McKenzie, with the plantings distributed throughout the season. Some are dumped at boat launches, but a large percentage are dispersed via a pontoon stocking boat rigged with a basket and a gate for a measured release rate, spreading the fish along an extended section of water. These fish are stocked from Paradise Campground down to Hayden Bridge, some 50 miles. There are additional stockings of 120,000 fin-clipped fish distributed among the South Fork above Cougar Reservoir, in Blue River, in the Leaburg pool above Leaburg dam, in Carmen and Trail Bridge Reservoirs and in Clear Lake.

◆

Although whitefish eggs are a pale translucent golden color and measure a little over 1mm in diameter, the author has had excellent success with pink or red yarn eggs 5 and 7mm in diameter.

Because of lower water temperatures in December, steelhead hug the bottom and are less likely to move more than a few inches to take your fly. It takes faith to be a December McKenzie steelheader.

Biologists are uncertain as to the impact that these fish have on the wild trout population in the mainstem McKenzie partly because of the tremendous number of anglers that ply her waters every year. Although anglers may use any method to catch their limit of five fin-clipped trout from the fourth Saturday in April until October 31 in the stretch from Paradise to Hayden, all non-fin-clipped (wild) trout must be released, including bull trout.

Biologists suspect that there are equal numbers of wild rainbow distributed throughout the McKenzie, but they have found many more cutthroat below Hayden Bridge. They attribute the higher cutthroat population in the lower river partly to the proximity of Hayden Bridge to the Mohawk, the prime cutthroat spawning tributary on the McKenzie (about a mile downstream from Hayden). Also, the lower river offers higher productivity due to increased amounts of nutrients and higher water temperatures.

Current regulations require release of all wild trout (and bull trout) on the McKenzie, with a bag limit of five fin-clipped trout per day. From the mouth (where the McKenzie joins the Willamette River) upstream to Hayden Bridge is open year round, barbless flies and lures only. From Hayden Bridge upstream to Paradise Campground is open from the fourth Saturday in April to October 31, any angling method. The section from Paradise upstream to Trail Bridge dam is also open from the fourth Saturday in April to October 31, but is restricted to barbless flies and lures only.

Biologists speculate that future years may bring additional barbless hook areas throughout the state, including the McKenzie, primarily to decrease hooking mortality of wild fish. This movement towards barbless hooks makes sense because it doesn't substantially reduce the harvest of hatchery fish, but very well may substantially reduce the damage to wild fish, primarily because a barbless hook makes it easier and quicker to turn fish loose. In fact, biologists are proposing an additional winter trout fishery from November 1st to the fourth Saturday in April in the section from Hayden Bridge upstream to Leaburg dam, barbless flies and lures.

The End of the Season

Snowflakes drift down, raising white shoulders on ranks of Douglas fir and river alder, cloaking the headwaters of the McKenzie while feeding the subterranean water closets deep in the lava rocks that form the backbone of the Cascades. Snowpack builds, covering iced-over lakes, buffering the ground from winter winds. While lake and forest sleep, trout metabolisms slow, allowing trout to subsist on midge larvae and pupae, snails and the occasional sluggish sculpin.

In the lower river, water levels rise as the river clouds with turbidity from rain mixed with snow runoff. Lowered water temperatures slow trout, compressing their feeding time to the midday hours, even when whitefish crowd the riffles to spawn.

Fishing days are few in December, though fishermen always look to the 'morrow, when the river is "in shape" and hatches bring trout to feed. But December is the time to remember the season past, read books, build rods, and tie flies.

The joy of fishing is stealing a day—feeling your most alive, smelling the river smells, watching osprey wheel and dive, wading the river, feeling the pull of the current against your legs, and then the pull of the trout on your rod.

I am at my most alive when fly fishing, whether the trout takes my nymph, strikes the dry in a splashy take, or a McKenzie steelhead strikes my fly, flooding my senses with adrenaline-enhanced excitement. The McKenzie is alive, too, plunging and flowing to join the Willamette, and later to mingle with the sea.

December is a time of musing, a speculation on the year as a circle of time, another year we witness the carousel of seasons, the comings and goings of birds, aquatic insects, cold, heat, rain and snow, and our own mingling with the river. I know that someday I will die, and that my bones will turn to dust, not that much unlike the volcanic dust that forms the riverbed that cradles the McKenzie. And as such, I will be a part of the river, just as much as I am a part of the river when I fish it. I like being a part of the McKenzie, and a fly rod is a great way to be there.

◆

Hatchery personnel use a dart gun to imbed a Floy anchor tag, a nylon "T-Bar", in the base of the dorsal fin, to mark re-released steelhead so they are not counted twice at the hatchery.

Snowflakes drift down, raising white shoulders on ranks of Douglas fir and river alder, cloaking the headwaters of the McKenzie.

Information Sources

Eugene/Springfield Convention & Visitors Bureau
115 W. 8th, Suite 190
PO Box 10286
Eugene, OR 97440
phone (541) 484-5307 or 1-800-547-5445

The Caddis Fly
168 W. 6th
Eugene, OR 97401
(541) 342-7005, FAX 503-342-6362

Homewaters Fly Fishing
444 W. 3rd Ave
Eugene, OR 97401
(541) 342-6691

McKenzie River Guides Association
Brad Edwards, President
90497 Mountain View Lane
Leaburg, OR 97489
(541) 896-3547

Oregon Department of Fish & Wildlife
Springfield District Office
3150 East Main Street
Springfield, OR 97478
(541) 726-3515

Willamette National Forest
Federal Building
211 East 7th Avenue
PO Box 10607
Eugene, OR 97440
(541) 465-6521
National Forest map, brochures on: Delta Old Growth Grove Nature Trail, Delta Campground; Lookout Creek Old-Growth Trail in H.J. Andrews Experimental Forest; Aufderheide National Scenic Byway Auto Tour, McKenzie River National Recreation Trail

Oregon State Parks & Recreation Department
1115 Commercial St. NE
Salem, OR 97310-1001
(503) 378-6305
Campsite Information Center, March to Labor Day
1-800-452-5687

Old Growth Day Hikes Maps
Willamette National Forest
PO Box 11288
Eugene, OR 97440

Oregon Tourism Division
775 Summer St. NE
Salem, OR 97310
1-800-547-7842
Oregon travel guide

Oregon Department of Transportation
140 Transportation Bldg.
Salem, OR 97310
(503) 986-3200
State highway map

With a Spey rod, Chris Daughters skirmishes with a steelhead, attempting to land it on that sandy beach.

If you want to coalesce with the McKenzie, take time out for gravel bars. Try sitting on a gravel bar without your rod, just listening to the river and looking around.